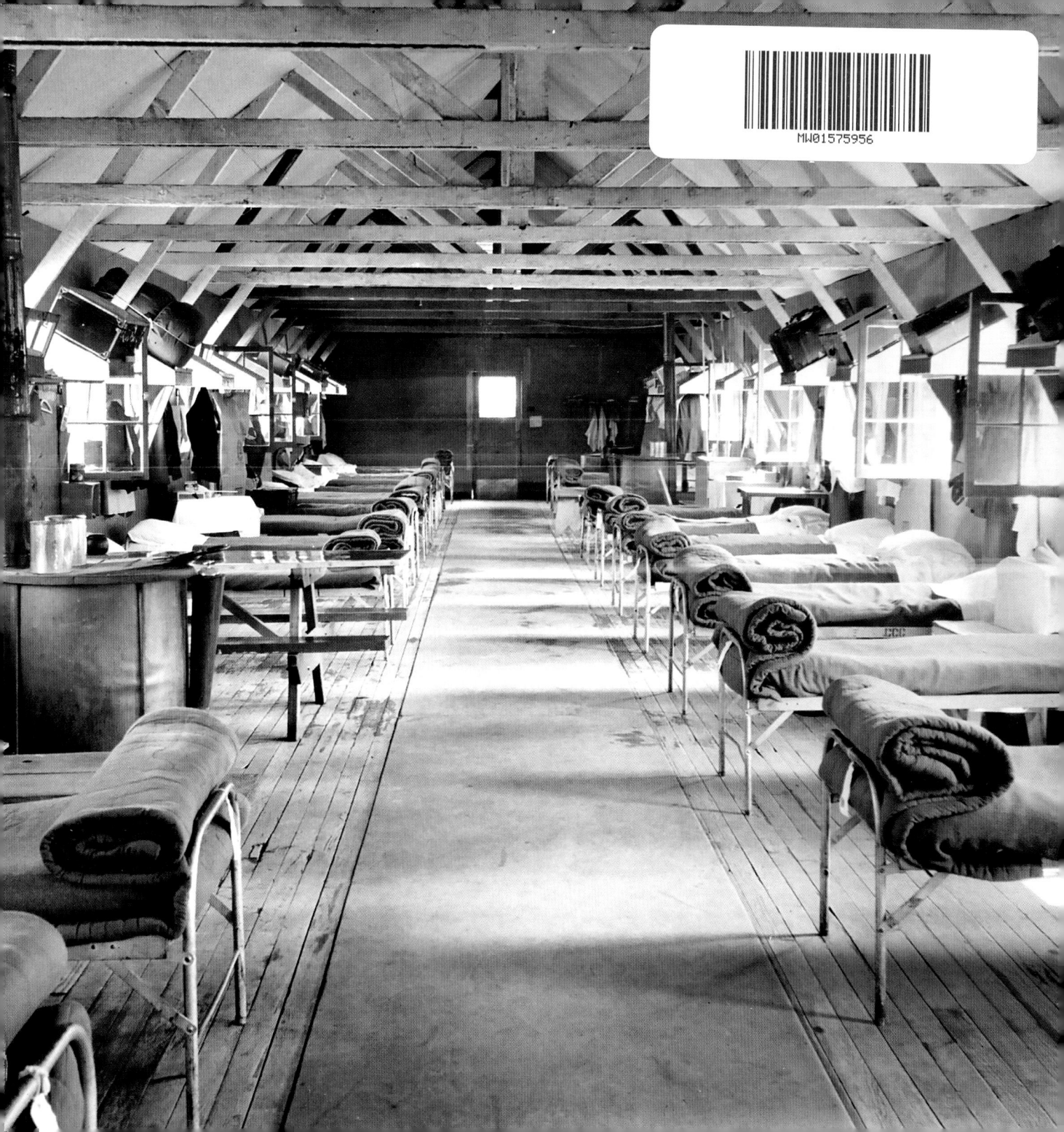

THE MISSION OF TUNA CANYON DETENTION STATION COALITION
IS TO PRESERVE THE STORIES OF THE JAPANESE, GERMANS, ITALIANS, JAPANESE TAKEN FROM PERU, AND OTHERS AT THE TUNA CANYON DETENTION STATION, WHICH WAS OPERATED BY THE U.S. DEPARTMENT OF JUSTICE DURING WORLD WAR II AND WAS LOCATED IN THE CITY OF LOS ANGELES.

FOR MORE INFORMATION PLEASE VISIT
www.tunacanyon.org

This publication was developed from a traveling exhibition created by
TUNA CANYON DETENTION STATION COALITION

THE EXHIBITION PROJECT WAS FUNDED, IN PART, BY A GRANT FROM THE U.S. DEPARTMENT OF THE INTERIOR, NATIONAL PARK SERVICE, JAPANESE AMERICAN CONFINEMENT SITES GRANT PROGRAM.

With special thanks to
THE FAMILY OF MERRILL SCOTT

Copyright © 2018 Tuna Canyon Detention Station Coalition

Images have been provided in many cases by the owners or custodians of the work. Individual works of art appearing herein may be protected by copyright in the United States of America or elsewhere, and may not be reproduced in any form without the permission of the rights holders. In reproducing the images contained in this publication, Tuna Canyon Detention Station Coalition obtained the permission of the rights holders whenever possible. In some instances, the Coalition was unable to locate a rights holder, notwithstanding good faith efforts. Tuna Canyon Detention Station Coalition requests that any contact information concerning such rights holders be forwarded so that they may be contacted for future editions.

All rights reserved. No part of the Tuna Canyon Detention Station story called *Only the Oaks Remain* may be reproduced or duplicated without prior written permission from the Tuna Canyon Detention Station Coalition.
First published in 2018 by Tuna Canyon Detention Station Coalition,
San Fernando Valley Japanese American Community Center, 12953 Branford Street, Pacoima, CA 91331.
Book and cover design by JCRR Design, Palm Springs, CA. Printed in the United States of America.
Library of Congress Control Number: 2017919379
ISBN: 978-0-9997570-0-0

ONLY THE OAKS REMAIN

The beauty of this oak grove belies a tragic history.
At the beginning of World War II, the U.S. Department of Justice
turned Civilian Conservation Corps Camp 902 into
the Tuna Canyon Detention Station by enclosing it
with barbed wire and posting armed guards.
From December 1941 to October 1943, Japanese, German,
and Italian immigrants, Japanese taken from Peru, and others
were imprisoned here in violation of their civil liberties.

On June 25, 2013, the Los Angeles City Council designated
this site as a Los Angeles Historic-Cultural Monument.
The oaks, as witnesses to history, compel us to learn
from our nation's mistakes and stand strong
against prejudice, wartime hysteria, and injustice.

A plaque like this will be installed at the site of the
Tuna Canyon Detention Station Historic-Cultural Monument

This book is dedicated to
Dr. William Lloyd Hitt, Paul Tsuneishi, and Richard Alarcon
whose tenacity made historical preservation of Tuna Canyon Detention Station possible.

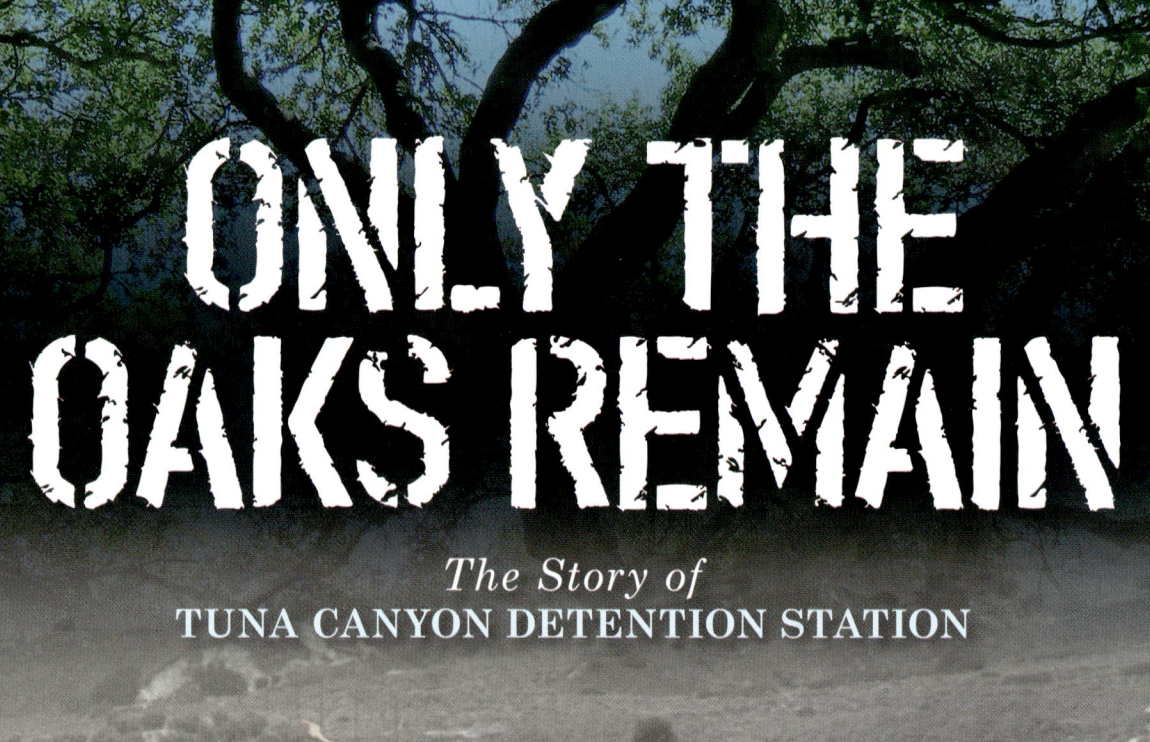

ONLY THE OAKS REMAIN

The Story of TUNA CANYON DETENTION STATION

Tuna Canyon Detention Station Coalition

CONTENTS

Honor Roll	Inside front cover
Introduction	pages 6–7
What Was Tuna Canyon Detention Station?	pages 8 – 21
How Was Detention/Internment Even Possible?	pages 22 – 35
Who Was at Tuna Canyon Detention Station?	pages 36 – 46
What Was It Like Being an Enemy Alien?	pages 47 – 61
Could Detention/Internment Happen Today?	pages 62 – 63
Acknowledgments	Inside back cover

Below
The guard control room at Tuna Canyon Detention Station
Courtesy of the Merrill Scott family

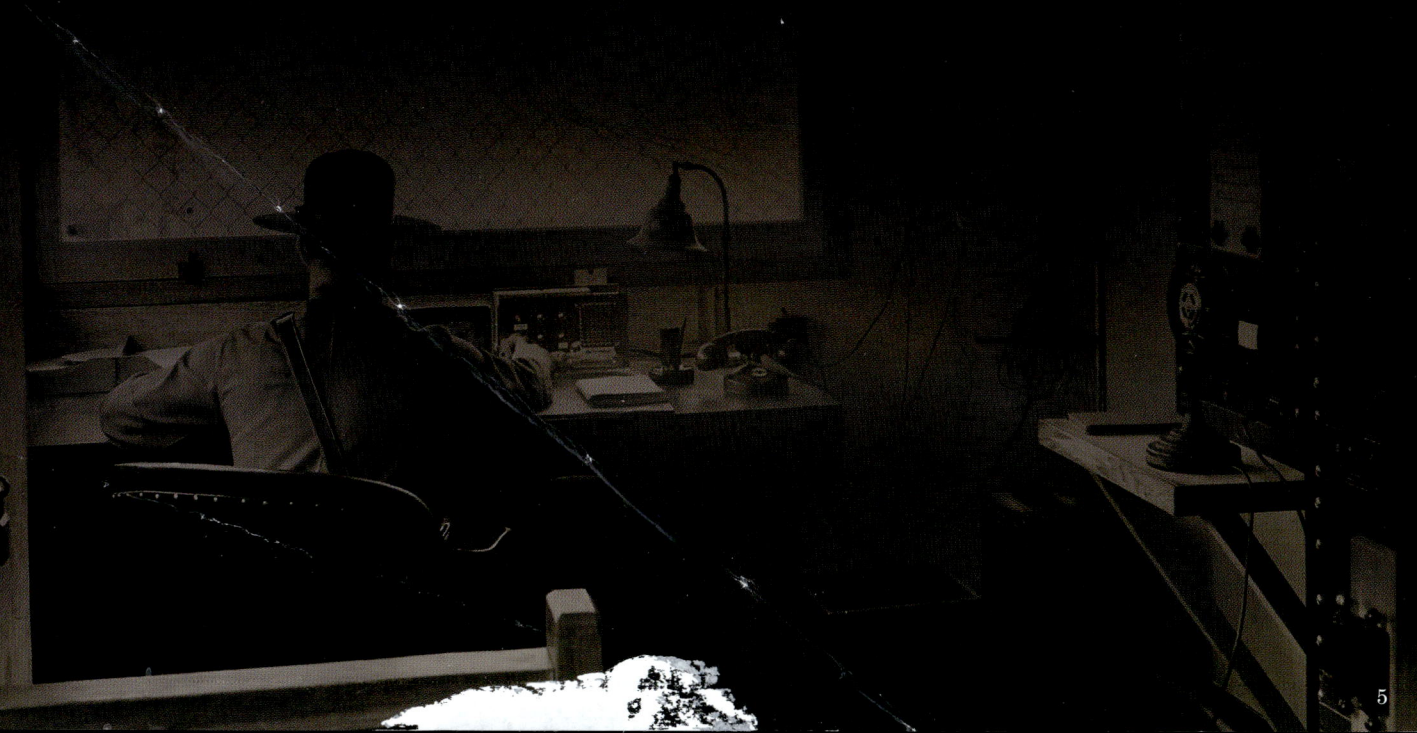

INTRODUCTION

In 2006, Dr. Lloyd Hitt and Paul Tsuneishi began examining World War II enemy alien documents newly released by the National Archives at Laguna Niguel, California (now located near Riverside). Thus, they began the journey to preserve the Tuna Canyon Detention Station's history.

On June 25, 2013, the Los Angeles City Council unanimously passed a motion introduced by Richard Alarcon, District 7 Councilman, to designate Tuna Canyon as a Los Angeles Historic-Cultural Monument. The community rose up to make this happen by writing letters, signing petitions, and making presentations.

The Tuna Canyon Detention Station Coalition was formed in 2014 as a nonprofit corporation. The primary mission of the Coalition is to tell the story of Tuna Canyon.

This story is about alien immigrant Japanese, German, and Italian leaders, Japanese taken from Peru, and others who were arrested beginning December 7, 1941 as alleged risks to national security. They were first imprisoned in local jails and then put into temporary Department of Justice detention stations like Tuna Canyon. Later, detainees were sent on to other facilities at places such as Ft. Missoula, Montana; Ft. Lincoln, South Dakota; Santa Fe, New Mexico; Stringtown, Oklahoma; McAlester, Oklahoma; and Kenedy, Texas.

The legal justification for such government actions came from the 1798 Alien Enemies Act signed by President John Adams, which was recodified in 1918. This legislation gave (and continues to give) the President the authority in time of war to arrest and confine, without trials, aliens from enemy nations. However, the government abused this authority, and during World War II, tens of thousands of innocent individuals were imprisoned.

The story of the arrest and confinement of enemy aliens is not as well known as the subsequent mass incarceration of West Coast Japanese Americans under Executive Order 9066. Some of this can be attributed to the fact that enemy alien prisoners were largely middle-aged community leaders at that time, and they have long since passed. For many years, the story of Tuna Canyon resided only in the hearts and minds of the detainees' descendants.

In 2015, the Coalition received a National Park Service Japanese American Confinement Sites (JACS) grant to build a traveling exhibit to tell the story of Tuna Canyon. *Only the Oaks Remain* was selected as the title of the exhibit because only the mature oaks and sycamores remain at the Tuna Canyon site. Dr. Kanji Sahara spearheaded the development of the traveling exhibit as the project director. Many scholars and community members contributed countless hours to produce and review the material. At first there was little information,

In the traveling exhibit, the Tuna Canyon story is told in 36 beautiful display panels, the content of which is reproduced in this book. There is also a diorama based on actual maps, painstakingly produced by Tatemono Construction. A key part of the exhibit are photographs provided by David Scott, the grandson of Tuna Canyon Officer-in-Charge Merrill Scott.

We thank the National Park Service JACS grant staff for believing in us. The inside back cover also lists the sponsors without whom this project would not have been possible. Special thanks go to the San Fernando Valley Japanese American Community Center, whose mission is to preserve the Japanese and Japanese American experience through education. We are grateful to JCRR Design who created the exhibit and this book.

An unfinished piece of business for the Coalition is to construct a memorial at the actual site of the Tuna Canyon Detention Station in Tujunga, a community that is part of the City of Los Angeles. When we begin the construction, we will want to again ask for support from our generous friends.

The story of the Tuna Canyon Detention Station is the story of the fragility of Constitutional and human rights. Through the traveling exhibit, a permanent memorial, and other work, we will continue to tell this story to help ensure that no other groups ever suffer such a loss of liberty and freedom.

TUNA CANYON DETENTION STATION COALITION

A Note about this Book

Following new conventions established by scholars and community activists, this book, and the exhibit on which it is based, uses the following terminology.

- After arrest, enemy aliens were sent to **detention stations**, like Tuna Canyon, as **detainees** before being transferred to **internment camps** as **internees**.
- During the subsequent mass incarceration of Japanese and Japanese Americans under Executive Order 9066, individuals were first sent to **detention centers**, such as Santa Anita, and then to ten **American concentration camps**, like Manzanar.
- This book, and the exhibit on which it is based, does not use government euphemisms such as **evacuation**, **assembly centers**, and **relocation camps**.

> "The Japanese are bombing Pearl Harbor. It's War. You may be able to hear it yourself. Listen!"
>
> Special Agent in Charge of the FBI's Honolulu office on the telephone to FBI Director J. Edgar Hoover, December 7, 1941

WHAT WAS TUNA CANYON DETENTION STATION?

U.S. involvement in World War II produced casualties, not only overseas in the battle zones, but also at home. A tragic abuse of civil and human rights was perpetrated against people of Japanese, German, and Italian ancestry in the U.S. and Latin America.

For them, the detention/internment system devised in the years leading up to World War II and implemented rapidly after the Imperial Japanese bombing of Pearl Harbor would be a painful demonstration that civil rights can be easily lost.

Tuna Canyon Detention Station was the first step along the road to learning that lesson.

Opposite
The USS Arizona (BB-39) burning after the Imperial Japanese attacks on Pearl Harbor, December 7, 1941
Photographer unknown [Public domain], via Wikimedia Commons

After the outbreak of the war and for several years thereafter, many arrested Japanese, German, and Italians were sent to Tuna Canyon before being transferred to other confinement sites. Enemy aliens were also subject to contraband, curfew, travel, and other restrictions.

```
FBI LOS ANGELES 12-7-41 11-32 PM GLB
DIRECTOR

Following additional Japanese have been apprehended, making to-
tal of ninety in custody.

Kouji Kikushima, Manroku Tatekawa, Kyutaro Yamamoto, Kamenosuke
Aoki, Sadaji Maikawa, Nisuke Yamahiro, Munekuma Sakuye, Daisuke
Hori, Gengoro Tonai, Yasutaro Tanaka, Kihei Tanaka, Hachizo
Matsuura, --Yatsuko--, Mrs. Satoko Kazahya, Shigenaga Kawata,
Tomoichi Uyeno, Tomiji Hirao, Gentaro Bessho, Masajiro Kai,
Mataji Yashii, Tsao Toshima, Asatoshi Takuwa, Shunichi Kishima,
Goro Hata, Tsao Haga.

Hood
END
OK FBI WASH ON
```

By 11:32 pm on December 7, 1941, ninety Japanese *Issei* had been arrested and taken into custody.
National Archives at Washington D.C.

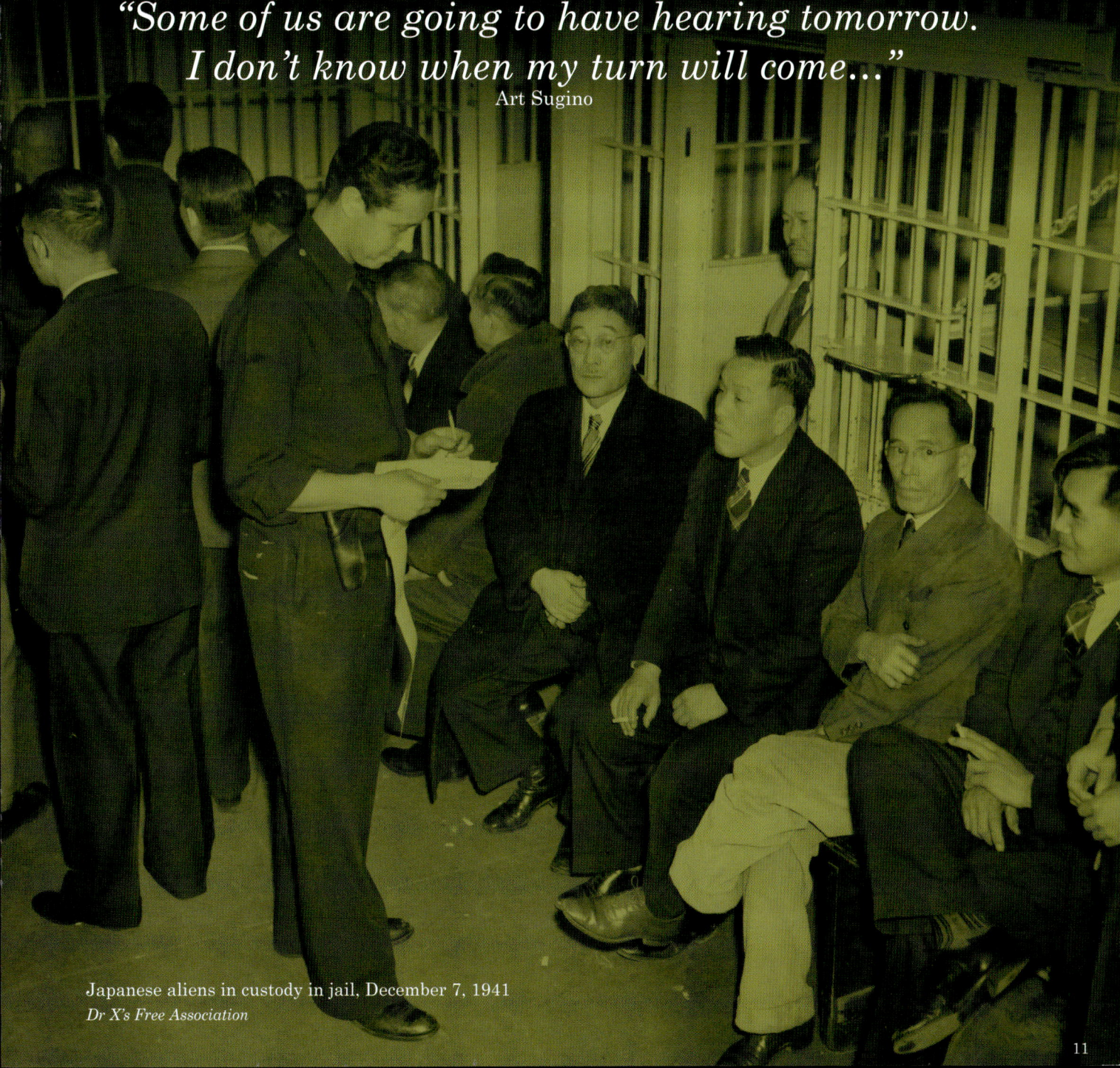

Japanese aliens in custody in jail, December 7, 1941
Dr X's Free Association

FBI agents and other law enforcement officials arresting Japanese in the first round of mass removals, December, 1941.

Los Angeles Daily News negatives collection, Department of Special Collections, Charles E. Young Research Library, UCLA

FIRST ARRESTS

"Cameras, radios capable of short wave reception, and firearms of all kinds flowed into police stations and Sheriff's substations throughout the city and county yesterday in an ever-increasing stream as enemy aliens complied with a government order that the first two articles be turned in."

Los Angeles Times, December 29, 1941

Searches for incriminating evidence were instigated in enemy alien homes throughout the United States.

Image courtesy of San Francisco Public Library

Several hundred male Terminal Island *Issei* fishermen were rounded up and detained by federal, city, and county officers, February 2, 1942.

Image courtesy of AP Photo/Ira W. Guldner

GATEWAY TO THE CAMPS

What started as arrests eventually led to the gates of the Tuna Canyon Detention Station for over 2,000 enemy aliens. With visits from family restricted to meetings on either side of the barbed-wire topped fences, little could have been known by its new incoming detainees of the fate that awaited them.

CASE STUDY: **Fritz Caspari** *German Scholar*

In 1933, Fritz Caspari was one of only two students from Germany to win a Rhodes Scholarship to Oxford University. A strong opponent of Hitler, Caspari spent the war years in what he called "voluntary political exile" in the United States where he taught German and history at Scripps College in Southern California.

The day after the bombing of Pearl Harbor, Caspari was arrested with the charge against him summarized as "German sympathies." Detained at San Pedro, he was released in February of 1942 but arrested again in September and detained at Tuna Canyon.

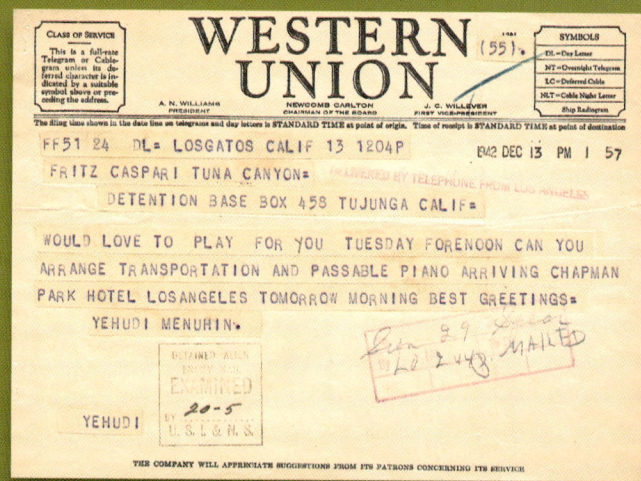

It was during this time that the acclaimed violinist Yehudi Menuhin wrote to Fritz offering to play at Tuna Canyon, though it is not certain this ever took place. At Tuna Canyon, Fritz became the mess officer and tried to ensure that all the detainees could obtain decent food in line with their cultural preferences.

Paroled in January of 1943, Caspari returned to Germany in 1954 to work in the German Foreign Service. He served as a Counsellor at the German Embassy in London, the Deputy Chief of the German Mission to the United Nations, and later as the German Ambassador to Portugal. He was knighted by Queen Elizabeth in 1972 and is remembered as Professor Sir Fritz Caspari.

Student. Scholar. Diplomat. And – not once, but twice – a prisoner.

Above left Tuna Canyon Detention Station guard post and entrance gate *Courtesy of the Merrill Scott Family*
Above right Telegram from Yehudi Menuhin to Fritz Caspari *Courtesy of the Caspari Family*

Tameji Eto
Los Osos (San Obispo County)
Courtesy of Naomi Shibata

Yataro Yamane
North Hollywood
Courtesy of Teddy Yamane

Renzo Cesana
Hollywood Hills
Courtesy of Alchetron

Charles Mitsuji Furuta
Wintersburg Village (Huntington Beach)
Historic Wintersburg, Furuta Family Collection

Fritz Caspari
Claremont
Scripps yearbook, "La Semeuse" 1940

Zentaro Asamen
Westmorland
Courtesy of Tim Asamen

WHAT WAS TUNA CANYON DETENTION STATION? 15

Tuna Canyon Detention Station sitting among a grove of oaks. Many of these oaks remain at the site.
Photograph courtesy of the Merrill Scott family

Tuna Canyon Detention Station

started life as a Civilian Conservation Corps (CCC) site in 1933. CCC camps were very popular with unemployed young men because they helped them finish high school and learn a trade while sending money home to their families. They worked to support the forestry department in fighting fires, planting trees and building roads, trails and campgrounds.

The Immigration and Naturalization Service (INS) commandeered the CCC camp on December 7, 1941. Ten foot high chain-link fence topped with barbed wire, flood lights, guard towers and a lookout tower on the northern ridge were added. The first prisoners entered the camp on December 16, 1941.

The detainees were primarily Japanese, German, and Italian aliens from Southern California and Japanese from Peru. The camp held them for processing. Most were then sent on to other Immigration and Naturalization confinement sites in Missoula, Montana, Bismarck, North Dakota, and Santa Fe, New Mexico. On two occasions, it was necessary to open temporary Tuna Canyon substations to accommodate the numbers of prisoners. These substations were located at the Army's internment site in Griffith Park, Los Angeles and at the Federal Correctional Institution on Terminal Island, San Pedro. The Tuna Canyon Detention Station was in operation until the end of October 1943. During its existence it processed over 2,000 enemy aliens, the majority of whom were Japanese.

The camp consisted of seven barracks, one infirmary, one mess hall, one administration building, and one office building. One of the barracks was a recreation building which included a library from the CCC camp.

1950 Photo of Los Angeles Probation Camp
(the former Tuna Canyon Detention Station)
Courtesy of Los Angeles Historical Aerials

Note: The long barracks were removed to make way for a basketball court

La Tuna camp, ca. 1934
Courtesy of Little Landers Historical Society at Bolton Hall Museum

The building was also used for Christian and Buddhist services and movies. Each barrack had an internee Captain. The Captains reported to the internee Mayor who reported to INS Officer in Charge Merrill Scott.

The Japanese supplied their own cooks and took care of cooking, serving and clean-up at the mess hall. The guards ate the same food in the same mess hall. The internees maintained the grounds including the gardens where they grew vegetables for the kitchen. The Infirmary was staffed by a local Tujunga doctor, who was on call. Most of the time there was a Japanese doctor being held at the camp who was preferred by the Japanese men.

Wednesday and Sunday were Visitation Days. Regulations required internees to stand ten feet from the fence but their families could approach the fence. The rule was that only English could be spoken. Most *Issei* spoke very little English so communicating was often stressful. One *Issei* wife, so stressed that she blurted out words in Japanese, quickly found a bayonet against her throat.

Amongst this turmoil there was one individual who went out of his way to make things easier. First Officer Merrill Scott, who carried out his duties to the letter, was always fair and kind. He told his friend Reverend Herbert Nicholson, a visiting Quaker minister who was a missionary in Japan, that if it were up to him he would let the prisoners go home to take care of their affairs. He knew they would be back by nightfall.

Recreation building (left), infirmary (in distance), with a barrack building just visible (right).

The recreation building.

The co-op.

Mess hall, as seen by the officer of the guard from his post

NOW, THEREFORE, I, FRANKLIN D. ROOSEVELT, as PRESIDENT of the United States and as Commander in Chief of the Army and Navy of the United States, do hereby make public proclamation to all whom it may concern...

The first words of Presidential Proclamation 2525

Left
The first page of Presidential Proclamation 2525

National Archives at Washington D.C.

HOW WAS DETENTION/ INTERNMENT EVEN POSSIBLE?

America's participation in World War I had produced an ordered set of plans ready for the disposition of individuals living within United States territories who were considered to be a threat. When war became inevitable on December 7, 1941, there was never any doubt by President Franklin D. Roosevelt or his advisers that aliens from countries hostile to the United States would be interned, nor was it a matter of concern as to the direction this policy might lead. Its immediate purpose was to protect the country and its citizens from "potential danger" and the attack on Pearl Harbor naturally left virtually no challenges to this policy. Its implementation seemed fully justified.

Presidential Proclamations 2525, 2526, and 2527, allowed the instant detention and incarceration of Japanese, German, and Italian aliens respectively. Signed by President Roosevelt on December 8, 1941, these documents were backdated to December 7, 1941, when the first arrests and detentions of enemy aliens had begun.

Opposite
President Franklin D. Roosevelt signing the Declaration of War against Japan, December 8, 1941
Abbie Rowe [Public domain], via Wikimedia Commons

THE POWER OF A PRESIDENT

Early American History and the Internment of Enemy Aliens

The **Alien Enemies Act of 1798** was one of four laws known as the Alien and Sedition Acts passed by the Federalists, and signed by President John Adams in 1798.

It declared:

"...whenever there shall be a declared war between the United States and any foreign nation or government... the President of the United States shall make public proclamation of the event, all natives, citizens, denizens, or subjects of the hostile nation or government, being males of the age of fourteen years and upwards, who shall be within the United States, and not actually naturalized, shall be liable to be apprehended, restrained, secured and removed, as alien enemies."

John Adams

Thomas Jefferson

The Federalists were afraid of the French Revolution and believed that immigrants would be disloyal in the event of war. The Alien and Sedition Acts were written to undermine Thomas Jefferson's Democratic-Republican Party that supported the French Revolution. Adams believed in a strong central government while Jefferson believed states should have more power.

The passage of these four acts made Americans realize the fragility of the U.S. Constitution and Bill of Rights. These Acts were extremely unpopular and ignited a firestorm of criticism. It was the main campaign issue in 1800 when Jefferson beat Adams for the Presidency.

War of 1812 and the Internment of Enemy Aliens

The Alien Enemies Act was first used against British aliens in the War of 1812. It was amended several times and now remains in effect as the **Enemy Alien Act of 1918**. The law goes into effect by a President's "Public Proclamation" – no role for Congress. The first sentence in President Roosevelt's Proclamation 2525 cites the 1918 act as the "Authority"

Puck magazine, August 9, 1899

World War I and the Internment of Enemy Aliens

Presidential Proclamation 1364, was signed by President Woodrow Wilson. In 1916, Wilson's campaign slogan was "He kept us out of the War". After he won the re-election, he quickly became pro-war. On April 6, 1917, U.S. declared war on Germany and Wilson issued Proclamation 1364 with words that would reappear in Executive Order 9066.

Woodrow Wilson

"An alien enemy shall not reside in or continue to reside in, to remain in, or enter any locality which the President may from time to time designate by Executive Order as a prohibited area in which residence by an alien enemy shall be found by him to constitute a danger to the public peace and safety..."

"Uncle Sam sees hyphenated voters and asks, 'Why should I let these freaks cast whole ballots when they are only half American.'" From, 1918 some 250,000 German-Americans had to register at their post office and carry their alien registration cards at all times.

A vigilante group, the American Protective League (APL), with 200,000 untrained amateur detectives were deputized as a semi-official part of the Bureau of Investigation (BOI). APL had branches in 600 cities; and spied on German immigrants and anyone with dissenting views. In a 3-day period, APL arrested 75,000 suspected draft dodgers in New York City. The BOI was the forerunner of the Federal Bureau of Investigation (FBI).

Under pressure, the cities of German, Nebraska became Garland and Berlin, Michigan became Marne. Restaurants changed sauerkraut to liberty cabbage and hamburger to liberty steak. Music by Beethoven, Bach and Mozart were considered disloyal. German-American churches were targeted as agents of Germany. Banned from mail were magazines expressing anti-war views.

Acts of violence increased dramatically in the spring of 1918. Suspects were forced to sing patriotic songs and kiss the flag. Mobs invaded homes, threatened and beat suspects. On April 4, 1918 in Collinsville, Illinois, German immigrant Robert Prager was hung from a tree. A jury deliberated 45 minutes and acquitted his killers.

During World War I, Proclamation 1364 was used to intern 2,048 German aliens including 29 musicians and the director of the Boston Symphony Orchestra.

Robert Prager

Wikimedia commons

World War II and the Internment of Enemy Aliens

Presidential Proclamations 2525, 2526, and **2527** were used to intern Japanese, German, and Italian aliens respectively. While the detention and internment of enemy aliens during World War II was legal, this exhibit shows how the government greatly abused its authority in its treatment of Japanese, Germans, and Italians.

World War II and Martial Law in Hawaii

With the declaration of Military Martial Law by Territorial Governor Joseph Poindexter on December 7, 1941 after a telephone call to President Roosevelt, confinement of enemy aliens in in the U.S. territory of Hawaii was handled entirely by military forces under Military Governor General Walter Short.

World War II and the Internment of Latin Americans

In January 1942, a Conference of Pan American Ministers of Foreign Affairs adopted a U.S. proposal (based on pre-war plans and agreements) to restrict, intern, and deport "potentially dangerous" enemy aliens from their nations for national and hemispheric security. The U.S. government orchestrated a scheme whereby deported aliens would enter U.S. jurisdiction without visas or passports and be interned under the Alien Enemies Act.

U.S. government memos reveal concerns about leaving "written evidence" showing the U.S. role in deportations and hostage exchanges. Years later, John K. Emmerson, the U.S. State Department official who organized the program in Peru, described it as "clearly a violation of human rights."

World War II and the Incarceration of U.S. Citizens

Executive Order 9066 (EO9066) was signed by President Franklin D. Roosevelt on February 19, 1942.

The document has the words:

"...to prescribe military areas in such places and of such extent as he or the appropriate Military Commander may determine, from which any or all persons may be excluded, and with respect to which, the right of any person to enter, remain in, or leave shall be subject to whatever restrictions the Secretary of War or the appropriate Military Commander may impose in his discretion..."

EO9066 was used to imprison "any and all persons" – both citizens and aliens. In the spring and summer of 1942, 120,000 Americans of Japanese ancestry from the West Coast were sent to detention centers and then to American concentration camps.

Franklyn D. Roosevelt

A SOPHISTICATED AND WELL-PLANNED SYSTEM

	Detention Stations / Internment Camps	Detention Centers / American Concentration Camps	Hawaii Camps
Who	15,000 German, Japanese, and Italian aliens	120,000 people of Japanese ancestry, of which two-thirds were U.S. Citizens	2,000 Japanese aliens and U.S. Citizens, and German and Italian aliens
From where	Throughout U.S.	All of California, parts of Oregon, Washington and Arizona	Hawaii
Authorization	Public Proclamations 2525, 2526 & 2527 for Japanese, German and Italian Aliens, December 8, 1941	Executive Order 9066 February 19, 1942	Military Martial Law December 7, 1941
How interned	Many under surveillance before the war FBI and other law enforcement agencies made individual arrests	Posted notices "All Persons of Japanese Ancestry" to report to departure points on certain days	Under surveillance before the war. Three-man arresting squads and arresting cards
Facility examples	Modified existing facilities Many were Civilian Conservation Corps camps or old Army forts - Angel Island, Tuna Canyon - Santa Fe, Crystal City	Fairgrounds Newly constructed camps in isolated and desolate locations - Santa Anita, Tanforan - Manzanar, Tule Lake	Existing jails Newly constructed sites - Sand Island - Honouliuli

Above Tuna Canyon Detention Station, looking north towards guard towers *Courtesy of the Merrill Scott family*

HOW WAS DETENTION/INTERNMENT EVEN POSSIBLE?   29

DETAINMENT/ INTERNMENT SCORE CARD

December 18, 1941

FBI Director J. Edgar Hoover usually reported to Attorney General Francis Biddle on the status of the Alien Enemy Control Program with an extensive table, that listed by the 58 FBI Field Offices, the number of arrest of Aliens and Citizens.

National Archives at Washington D.C.

National Archives at Washington D.C.

By December 18, 1941 Hoover was able to report that a total of 2,903 Japanese, Italian, and German aliens had been taken into custody since Presidential Proclamations 2525, 2526, and 2527 allowed their arrest.

30   ONLY THE OAKS REMAIN

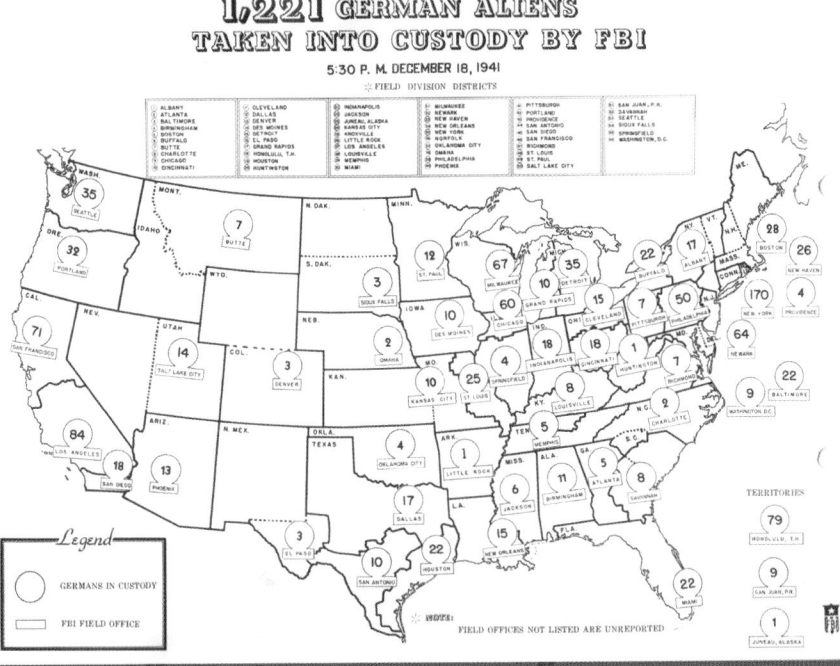

Maps accompanying his letter demonstrated that, after New York, Los Angeles had the second largest total of arrests at 409.

By May, 1943 total arrests in Los Angeles stood at 2,383, and at 13,603 for the whole of the country.

HOW WAS DETENTION/INTERNMENT EVEN POSSIBLE?

ROUND-UP CASE HISTORY: TERMINAL ISLAND

The Japanese Terminal Island (TI) community consisted of *Issei* fishermen and their families. Many *Issei* came from Wakayama Prefecture in Japan. Terminal Island was a tightly-knit island village of 3000 with a strong sense of hometown spirit and its own language, a unique combination of English and Japanese. Most residents worked on the approximately 250 fishing boats or in the local canneries.

As World War II began, Terminal Island *Issei* were suspected of being spies or saboteurs since they lived near important military and harbor facilities. Also because they knew the Pacific coastal waters well and had two-way radios, there was fear that they could aid Imperial Japanese military operations against the U.S. Mainland.

Control of Terminal Island *Issei* fishermen was a high government priority. Many returning to Terminal Island with their catch were detained. Those already at there were prevented from leaving. Just after Pearl Harbor, the FBI and other government agents arrested ninety-one fishermen who would later be sent to the Tuna Canyon Detention Station. On February 2, 1942, the FBI conducted a mass roundup of hundreds of Terminal Island *Issei* fishermen. Over 125 were sent to the San Pedro Detention Station and then to Tuna Canyon.

Courtesy Los Angeles Herald Examiner

Terminal Island *Issei* fishermen were a significant part of the imprisoned population at Tuna Canyon. But the Terminal Island Japanese community would experience a greater tragedy. On February 25, 1942, after the issuance of Executive Order 9066 by President Roosevelt, the remainder the Japanese Terminal Island community was given 48 hours notice to leave the island. A majority of the population was sent to the Manzanar Concentration Camp. Terminal Island Japanese lost their homes, belongings, businesses, and most of all their way of life.

POLICE AID FBI IN GIGANTIC ROUNDUP

A gigantic roundup designed to net 500 Japanese aliens was sprung suddenly and swiftly just before dawn today on Terminal Island, vital naval center in Los Angeles Harbor.

More than 150 G-men, police detectives and deputy sheriffs in plainclothes, moving with careful co-ordination and timing, swarmed onto the long island armed with "presidential warrants" from Washington, D. C., and began taking the Japanese fishermen and cannery workers into custody from their homes clustered about Fish Harbor.

The alien Japanese will be held under the presidential warrants pending hearings before enemy alien boards, according to J. W. Vincent, assistant chief of the Federal Bureau of Investigation, who was in charge of the drive.

Later, he said, those aliens whom the boards do not release will be given "an opportunity to decide between leaving the country and being interned for the duration."

The aliens were booked as "en route to the Immigration Office." Vincent said this latest and most dramatic move to combat the danger of Fifth-Column sabotage and espionage was "the result of a carefully planned and well-thought-out program."

As the roundup got rapidly under way, the drawbridge to the island was raised to prevent escape to the mainland of any of the aliens scheduled to be taken into custody.

Tension and drama marked the move on Terminal Island, site of Reeves Field, naval air base, in-

(Continued on Page 2, Column 6)

Los Angeles Herald Examiner
February 2, 1942
Courtesy Los Angeles Herald Examiner

cluding its seaplane landing, and location of an Edison Co. power plant and numerous shipping docks. Approximately 2100 Japanese live on th island, about 800 of them aliens. Nearly all the Japanese are either cannery workers or members of the Japanese fishing fleet, and a public rumor often has had it that Japanese naval officers in innocent disguise were members of that fleet.

In today's raids an F. B. I. agent would rap on the door of a fisherman's tiny house accompanied by two other officers, either police detectives or sheriff's deputies. Asking for the person named in their warrant, they would walk inside, wait until he had dressed, bring him out and put him in an automobile.

WEEPING WIFE

A Mrs. Saito leaned out the door of her cottage and wept loudly as her husband was led away, not knowing where he was being taken or when he would return. The scene was typical as families were separated by wartime's harsh precautions.

One door was opened by a tiny youngster in response to the knock of officers, who asked, "Where's papa?"

"He's asleep," said the child.

"That's all right, we'll come in," said the officers, entering as they spoke.

The officers awakened their man and waited while he ate breakfast.

OMINOUS ATMOSPHERE

Officers about to undertake the roundup stood in knots on street corners, and Japanese youngsters walking to school looked them over apprehensively, knowing something ominous was in the air.

The tiny wooden homes of the Japanese are so crowded together there is barely room to walk between on the narrow brick alleyways in some sectors. The structures have their backs to the streets and their fronts face together across the narrow passageways.

Seeing a man who might be a Japanese alien on the street, officers would tell him to go home and wait. As the raids progressed, American fishermen nearby went calmly ahead cleaning their nets.

Only men were taken into custody, and Japanese women and children were told to remain in their homes.

The roundup apparently was the government's answer to the question—"What's to be done about Terminal Island?"—which has arisen since enemy aliens last week were ordered ousted from 13 "prohibitive zones," not, however, including Terminal Island.

CAREFULLY PLANNED

The move was carried out with precise teamwork and careful, secret preparation by the arresting officers.

Police and sheriff's deputies were called in to aid in the roundup by agents of the Federal Bureau of Investigation.

Ninety police detectives met at their Los Angeles City Hall headquarters before dawn and commanded by Inspector Bruce Clark and Capt. Vern Rasmussen were dispatched, two to a radio car, to Terminal Island.

HOW WAS DETENTION/INTERNMENT EVEN POSSIBLE?

"A, B, C" LISTS AND THE CUSTODIAL DETENTION INDEX (CDI)

During the 1930's the U.S. government became increasing concerned about threats to internal security posed by Japanese, Germans, and Italians in the U.S. It began compiling lists of what were seen as suspicious organizations and individuals. These lists would be used to decide who would be imprisoned if war broke out with Axis powers. The best known were the FBI's custodial detention lists started in 1939.

Such lists ranked organizations and individuals in terms of the potential danger they were thought to pose. Three main categories, A, B, and C, were used with A being the most dangerous.

J. Edgar Hoover, Director of the FBI, devised the Custodial Detention Index between 1939 and 1941 to determine who to keep under surveillance and who to arrest in the event of war

The FBI had a list of "subversive organizations", for example, the Japanese Imperial Army Veterans organization, as well as "...extensive indices of individuals, groups, and organization engaged in subversive activities, in espionage activities, or any activities that are possibly detrimental in the internal security of the U.S...."

Each person was on two individual index cards arranged alphabetically and geographically. Hoover claimed he could find any enemy alien from them.

Marion S. Trikosko, Library of Congress Prints & Photographs Division

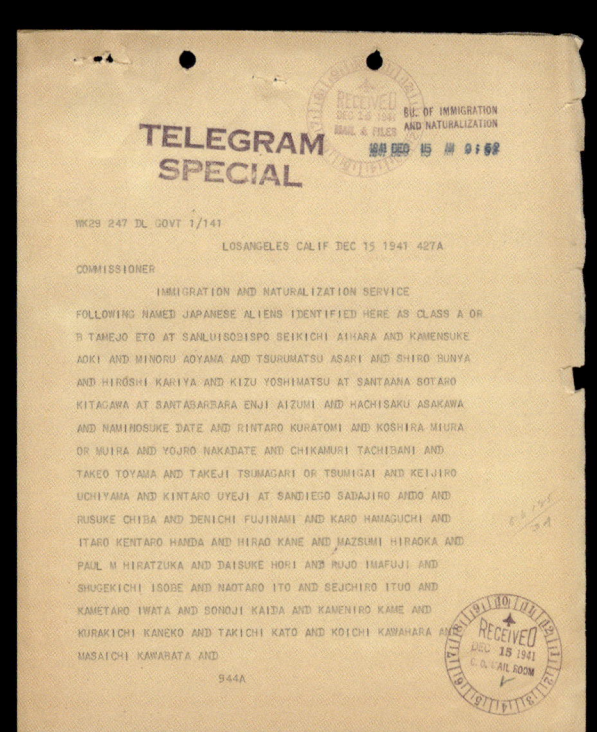

The lists were therefore known as ABC lists. A custodial detention index provided specific criteria for these categories.

During the war, the FBI and other agencies used ABC lists to arrest thousands of innocent immigrants such as prominent businessmen, religious leaders, fishermen, community organization members, language school teachers, and newspaper editors.

Telegrams detailing "A" list enemy aliens
National Archives at Washington D.C.

Francis Biddle, Attorney General from August, 1941 to June, 1945, to whom the FBI reported.
On July 6, 1943, Biddle found out about the Custodial Detention Index for American citizens. Biddle said:

"There is no statuary authorization or other present justification for keeping a "custodial detention list" of citizens. It is now clear to me that this classification system is inherently unreliable."

In July of 1943 Biddle ordered FBI Director Hoover to abolish the Custodial Detention Index.

First Officer Merrill Scott with Otoji Hara, grandfather of retired L.A.P.D. Deputy Chief, Terry Hara

Courtesy of the Merrill Scott family

A vase and box presented to Merrill Scott by grateful internees of Tuna Canyon Detention Station in 1942

WHO WAS AT TUNA CANYON DETENTION STATION?

Many of the stories of the people
who passed through the gates of Tuna Canyon Detention Center
have been lost forever.

The deprivation of freedom for the internees was a hard burden for
many, and for those who had undergone many sacrifices to come to the
United States, a bitter blow from which they would never recover.

These pages tell a few of the stories that have endured.

As proof that in such times humanity and compassion can still be
strongly present, two stories, not of internees, but of the people who
oversaw their needs while incarcerated, are here included.

Merrill Scott

FIRST OFFICER

In December of 1941, **Merrill Scott** was appointed the First Officer of Tuna Canyon Detention Station, a former Civilian Conservation Corps camp in Tujunga. He oversaw the conversion of the camp to a detention facility. A ten-foot chain link fence topped with barbed wire was erected, along with guard towers.

Scott showed a deep respect and understanding for the prisoners in his care. His instruction to the internees was;

"When the nations of Japan and the United States become belligerents, we Americans are naturally 100 percent patriotic for the United States. But you are citizens of Japan, and it is unavoidable that you feel for your country. But let's set aside that matter, and I want you to consider this place within the fence our home together and cooperate with us."

SCAN THIS QR CODE TO READ A MORE COMPLETE BIOGRAPHY OF MERRILL SCOTT

Barbed wire fence, locked gates
Do we stand inside or out
Truth lies on one side

SCAN THIS QR CODE TO HEAR DAVID SCOTT TALK ABOUT HIS GRANDFATHER

First Officer Merrill Scott in 1942
Courtesy of the Merrill Scott family

Herbert Nicholson was considered to be a man of inspirational love and unselfish service designed to improve the welfare of persons of Japanese ancestry. As a lifelong member of the Society of Friends he made his mission one to be devoted to the good of mankind.

The Nicholsons, people led by God, were often in dangerous situations and with very little funding. As a man who preached in churches, spoke the Japanese language, who intervened in the lives of those who needed comfort and spiritual guidance, he was loved by many. His Bible messages became alive and with real meaning. He was a man the Japanese looked to for joy, hope and love through those turbulent years of World War II.

He alone spoke up
Against Incarceration
In the hour of need

Reverend Nicholson with his family in 1949

From Valiant Odyssey by Herbert Nicholson. Self-published, 1978

SCAN THIS QR CODE TO READ A MORE COMPLETE BIOGRAPHY OF REVEREND NICHOLSON

Nikuma Tanouye was born in 1886 in Kumamoto, Japan. He completed high school, then came to America in 1903 and took up truck farming in Torrance, California. He was a Kendo Instructor. In 1918 Momoe Uemura came from Japan to become his wife. They had five children, who excelled in school. During WWI, Nikuma registered for the draft and was willing to serve for his adopted country.

Nikuma Tanouye, arrested and detained and en route to Tuna Canyon Detention Station, February 20, 1942

Courtesy Los Angeles Public Library, Herald Examiner Collection

On February 19, 1942 President Roosevelt signed Executive Order 9066. The next day, Tanouye's eldest son Ted was inducted into the Army. The following night Tanouye's world completely fell apart. In a midnight raid, the FBI kicked open the door of his home, raided the house and arrested him. This brought great shame to the family. He was interned in Tuna Canyon Detention Station. The most likely reason for Nikuma Tanouye's internment was because he taught Kendo.

During WWII, Nikuma's eldest son Ted was killed in action in Italy. Sergeant Tanouye received the Congressional Medal of Honor posthumously in 2000. During the Korean War, Nikuma's youngest son Yukiwo was also killed in action. Another son Isao, also fighting in Korea, accompanied his brother home and then returned to the front line to continue fighting for his country.

Technical Sergeant Ted Tanouye

U.S. CITIZEN, SON

Though not an internee at Tuna Canyon Detention Station, **Ted Takayuki Tanouye** was the eldest son of Nikuma and Momoe Tanouye. He made Honor Roll at Torrance High School, lettered in baseball and football each of his high school years and was Sophomore Class President. He was inducted into the Army and joined the 442nd Regimental Combat Team. For his bravery on Hill 140 south of the Arno River in Italy, he was awarded the Congressional Medal of Honor.

Ted's best friend in high school was Akira Shimatsu who was the first *Nisei* from Torrance to be killed in Italy. Ted Tanouye was the second. They had a joint Buddhist service and are buried side by side at Evergreen Cemetery in Los Angeles. Evergreen was one of the few cemeteries that would accept Japanese.

A drawing of Technical Sergeant Ted Tanouye
Courtesy Fallen Heroes Project

Dad suffers arrest
Family moved to barracks
Son a war hero

Courtesy of the Merrill Scott family

SCAN THIS QR CODE TO READ A MORE COMPLETE BIOGRAPHY OF NIKUMA TANOUYE AND HIS SON, TECHNICAL SERGEANT TED TANOUYE

Reverend Daisho Tana

BUDDHIST PRIEST & JAPANESE LANGUAGE SCHOOL TEACHER

Reverend Tana and his wife, the tanka poet, Tomoe Tana, with their family, ca. 1955.
Courtesy of Akira Tana

Buddhists in Japan long held the idea of *bukkyo tozen*, literally "the eastward transmission of Buddhism," to denote the geographic advance of their religion from its roots in India, across China, to Japan and then to the Americas.

Rev. Daisho Tana was first interned in Tuna Canyon and then Lordsburg and Santa Fe, New Mexico. His diary discusses the concept of *bukkyo tozen*: "It brings tears to my eyes to think of the profound words 'the eastward transmission of Buddhism' as I reflect on the fact that Buddhists on the Pacific coast have carried the Buddha all the way here to a place where we can see the Rocky Mountains as we celebrate the birth of the Buddha. While it may be true that the Buddhist organizations on the Pacific Coast have been decimated, the Buddha seeds that have now flown on the winds of this war will eventually move eastward and take root themselves before flowering into authentic Dharma flowers."

Amida Buddha
Chanting during O-higan
In Tuna Canyon

SCAN THIS QR CODE TO READ PAGES FROM REVEREND TANA'S DIARY

ONLY THE OAKS REMAIN

Kishiro Hayashi
JAPANESE PERUVIAN

25-year old **Kishiro Hayashi** was arrested because, as a factory and store manager, his name was on the Blacklist. He and over a hundred Japanese men were taken from jail and driven by truck out of the city. With destination and fate unknown and separated from his pregnant wife, Mr. Hayashi stated,

"I have no word to describe this utterly cruel treatment."

Three days later, they arrived at a harbor. Mr. Hayashi recalled,

"American soldiers with bayonets urged us to move…to the ship as if we were some animals….The military cargo ship set sail to Panama. Finally, it was clear that we were not going to be sent to the remote area in Peru, but were being sent to [the] US.

Onboard ship from Panama to [the] US,…I was assigned to clean the deck, but sometimes we were mistreated by a mean soldier who [kept] yelling at us, "Hurry up! Hurry up! and continuously poured hot water from behind us. It was a mean treatment."

Kishiro Hayashi ca. 1995
Courtesy of Enemy Alien Files

Taken from their home
In the land of the Incas
For hostage exchange

Courtesy of the Merrill Scott family

SCAN THIS QR CODE TO READ
A MORE COMPLETE BIOGRAPHY
OF KISHIRO HAYASHI

Cesare Grimaldi

ITALIAN ALIEN

When **Cesare Rene Grimaldi** was 25, he left his native Rome and emigrated to the United States. The year was 1928, and Benito Mussolini's tyranny was growing.

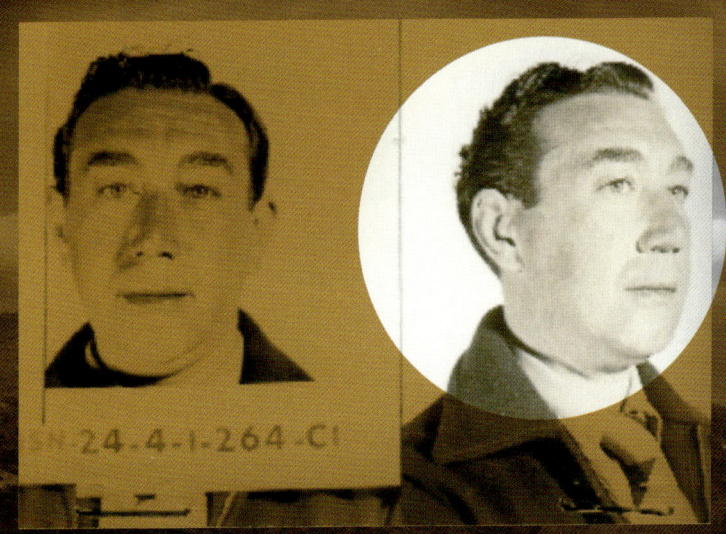

College educated with an ability to speak Italian, English, Spanish, and French, Grimaldi was admitted to the United States legally under an immigration quota and secured a position with the Italian consulate.

While working for the consulate in Los Angeles, he met California-born Corrinne Ross Harris. They were married on July 26, 1938 and three years later had a son whom they named Gian. Attracted by the emerging Hollywood film industry, Cesare left the consulate and found work as personal assistant to a movie director.

On December 8, 1941, FBI agents arrested Grimaldi, leaving his wife, Corinne, and six-month old son to fend for themselves. Transferred from one internment facility to another, Grimaldi wound up at Tuna Canyon Detention Center on May 26, 1943. By the time he was released in October 1943 he had spent almost two years in confinement.

Cesare Grimaldi in a government mugshot in 1941

Courtesy of National Archives at College Park

A Son of Roma
In Search of Liberty's Dream
Torn from His Loved Ones

SCAN THIS QR CODE TO READ A MORE COMPLETE BIOGRAPHY OF CESARE GRIMALDI

Dr. Eugen Banzhaf, Ph.D.
GERMAN IMMIGRANT

In 1927 **Dr. Eugen Banzhaf**, a Ph.D. in Civil Engineering, came to America from Germany as a sales representative for a German company. Two years later his intended, Emmy Ahrend, arrived and they were married. They made their home in Los Angeles where their only child, a daughter, was born in 1937. The couple applied for U.S. Citizenship.

On the night of December 7th, 1941 to the sound of screaming air-raid sirens, Eugen was apprehended at his home by the FBI. There was no explanation given as to where he would be taken. His whereabouts were not announced for a tension-filled three weeks.

Dr. Banzhaf with his wife and daughter in 1941
Courtesy Dr. Sigrid Toye

Eugen's arrest left his wife and daughter without means of support, all of his business and bank accounts having been frozen by the government. Emmy found it impossible to find work because no one would hire a 'Nazi-German' – a term used to refer to individuals of German descent. A fear gripped the population that such persons could be potential saboteurs – spitting on a German was even considered a patriotic gesture. The psychological ramifications of Emmy's experiences were extensive and included occasional hospitalizations. As a result, she was forced to abandon her child to be housed with strangers.

SCAN THIS QR CODE TO READ A MORE COMPLETE BIOGRAPHY OF DR. EUGEN BANZHAF

Heigoro Endo

FISHERMAN

Issei made major contributions to the growth of a large California fishing industry. **Heigoro Endo** was part of this story. He was 15 when he left Shizuoka-ken in 1900 and came to the United States. After a succession of jobs, he worked on fishing boats sailing from Terminal Island and then as the captain of his own tuna boat based at Wilmington. Later, he started a pioneering sportfishing business at White Point, San Pedro.

At the outbreak of World War II, the U.S. government considered *Issei* fisherman to be a danger to the security of the Pacific Coast. Heigoro faced additional suspicions because of his affiliation with Compton Gakuen, a well-known Japanese language school.

On March 30, 1942, Heigoro's family was given an order by the Army to leave their home within six days as part of the mass incarceration of West Coast Japanese. But two days later, he was suddenly arrested by the FBI without a warrant and detained at Tuna Canyon Detention Station.

At his hearing, Heigoro was not allowed to have legal counsel. The government made numerous false accusations about his complicity with the enemy — he was presumed to be guilty unless he could prove his innocence. Other arrested enemy aliens had similar experiences. Heigoro was later incarcerated with his family at Santa Anita and Jerome.

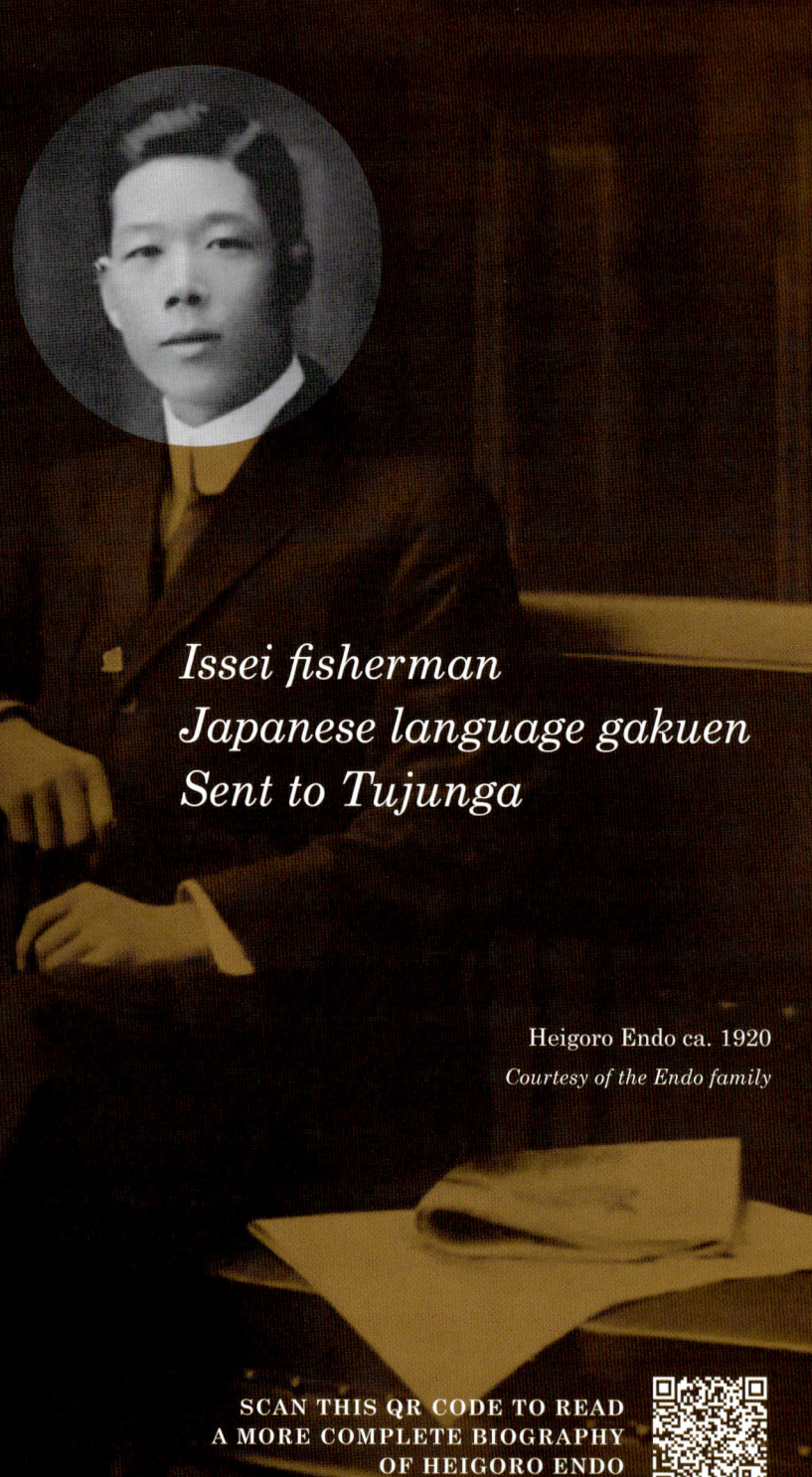

Issei fisherman
Japanese language gakuen
Sent to Tujunga

Heigoro Endo ca. 1920
Courtesy of the Endo family

SCAN THIS QR CODE TO READ
A MORE COMPLETE BIOGRAPHY
OF HEIGORO ENDO

WHAT WAS IT LIKE BEING AN ENEMY ALIEN?

"We used to have so much freedom and living in this country so long that we never felt we are foreigner until this war start and upset everything when we are called enemy alien. Now I am living as an enemy alien..."

Kenzo Sugino, in a letter to his wife, Chica

TOMOE TANA

Born in Hokkaido in 1913, Tomoe Tana immigrated to the United States after marrying Daisho Tana, a Shin Buddhist minister. During the tumultuous World War II period, Tomoe became separated from her husband when the two were sent to different camps. After the war, Tomoe became a U.S. citizen and received a master's degree from San Jose State University while pursuing her interest in tanka poetry. In 1949, she won Japan's Imperial Poetry contest, eventually emerging as an internationally recognized tanka poet and a leading proponent of the art form.

Me akureba ottono kao ari, tojinureba,
    matashimo ukabu ottowa waga mono

Open my eyes and there is the face of my husband,
    close them and I still see him, he is mine.

Kakuremino wareni ataeyo tsubasa mata,
    ottoga fusu yadoni waga tazunemunni

Give me a cloak and wings also,
    and I will visit where my husband sleeps.

Kokoro shiite tsuyoku tamotedo kainakute,
    yoni hiruni tayurutowa senu tsumano bonno

Trying hard to keep my heart strong in vain,
    night and day the desires of wife never cease.

Futo mezame, ottono hitomino nubatamano
    yamini semaruto omoedo munashiku

Waking up at night, thinking that
    the eyes of my husband are close, but in vain.

Poem written by Tomoe Tana to her husband while he was in Tuna Canyon Detention Station, March, 1942.

Courtesy of Akira Tana. Translation by Dr. Duncan Ryuken Williams.

Oaks at the site of Tuna Canyon Detention Station today.
Courtesy of William D. Skiles

HARUMATSU HINO

In 1917, at the age of 17, Harumatsu Hino traveled from Wakayama, Japan to Lompoc, California. Later, he, his wife, Ei, and two children, Yukio and Hanaye settled in Phoenix, Arizona and eventually moved to Los Angeles where Mitsugi and Teruo were born. Harumatsu Hino was arrested by the FBI on March 13, 1942 for serving as Treasurer of the San Fernando Valley Japanese Language School. While incarcerated in Santa Fe, New Mexico, he wrote haiku poems recalling his incarceration, how he coped, and his hopes for the future. The English translation of his poem is displayed below.

JOSEPH FRANK JACKISCH

With the U.S. entry into World War II, Joseph Frank Jackisch, born in Glasendorf, Germany in 1881, became one of 11,507 persons of German ancestry arrested and detained by the FBI as enemy aliens. Jackisch was living in Los Angeles at the time and working as a utility man. He had been in America since May 1916 and had renounced his allegiance to the German empire as early as 1922. His wife Elizabeth, whom he married in 1931, was also arrested. They had no children. Shortly after his release from custody, Jackisch registered for the U.S. draft.

NEW YEAR'S EVE IN CAMP TUJUNGA

We are together here
For a few hours
In Camp Tujunga
We ad some showers,
Now we have sunshine;
We have no beer or wine
(:In Camp Tujunga:)

Friends of this gathering
Let's all be merry,
It would be easier
With Tom and Jerry.
Time is fast passing away,
Soon it will be New Year's day
(:In Camp Tujunga:)

Nineteen and Forty Two
Is fast us leaving,
It was quite often sick,
Did lots of grieving.
Fare well to you old dear,
We will not shed a tear
(:In Camp Tujunga:)

Nineteen and Forty Three
The new born baby
Has plenty in store for us,
Not all will be gravy;
Whatever our fate,
Let us now celebrate
(:In Camp Tujunga:)

Grandpa Hino's Poem
Written end of May, 1942
Santa Fe Federal Prison

Thinking back, it was mid-Spring
Friday, March 13th when Father (he)
was arrested by the FBI and taken away.
The car passed through the Springs wind.
The men were cold and heartless.
Father (He) looked back many times.

With tears in his eyes, he watched the house,
and his dear wife and darling children.
His wife looked sad and as he closed his eyes,
He could still see her sadness and Father (he) cried.

It was the first time he had ever seen a prison,
and the sound of the door closing make him shutter.
The guards questioned him coldly.
Outside it stormed and inside him it also stormed—
he was sad and blue.
He cried silently inside himself yet consoled his wife and children.
Don't worry he thought our grief will soon disappear.

Beneath the cold skies of Tujunga, he way his family during visitation—
two times, three minutes at a time.
Every moment with his wife and children was precious.
And with each parting his heart broke to 1,000 pieces.

But the days passed quickly and soon it was May in Santa Fe.
He saw the trees and plants grow as todays became yesterdays.
Better not to think too much and better not to cry.
Under the dim light he waited for a letter from his wife.
The moon sat amongst the clouds and smiled down on him giving light.

What began as a tragedy became a fortune for the many friends he acquired.
And so he endured his time with less difficulty.
To his wife and children he hoped for peace and serenity,
as he knew the dawn of the day of his release would come.
He looked up toward a light giving him inner peace.
Wife and Children: the day will come when we will be together again,
and we will talk all night and share our past dreams.

Courtesy of Mitsu Hino

Tujunga Camp, Tujunga Camp,
How art thou now deserted?
The crowds who used to be out here
Are mostly gone, have Christmas cheer –
Tujunga Camp, Tuhunga Camp,
How are thou now deserted?

Tujunga Camp, Tujunga Camp,
Of those who still here ailing
A number east and sleep all day,
The others little work and play –
Tujunga Camp, Tujunga Camp,
Of those who still here ailing.

Tujunga Camp, Tujunga Camp,
Thy pretty dress remaining,
The mountains still around thee are,
But what we need here is a bar,
Tujunga Camp, Tujunga Camp,
Thy pretty dress remaining.

Tujunga Camp, Tujunga Camp,
Of cats here are aplenty:
They do not like on mice to feed,
But what they want is milk and meat:
Tujunga Camp, Tujunga Camp,
Of cats here are aplenty.

Tujunga Camp, Tujunga Camp,
No sin is here committed;
No liquor in the Camp you find –
Nor any women if you mind
Tujunga Camp, Tujunga Camp,
No sin is here committed.

Tujunga Camp, Tujunga Camp,
We will thee long remember.
Some day we all be gone from here,
The camp will then be lonesome there:
Tujunga Camp, Tujunga Camp,
We will thee long remember.

Courtesy of Dr. Sigrid Toye

REVEREND DAISHO TANA

Diary translated by
Dr. Duncan Ryuken Williams

Shin Buddhist minister Reverend Daisho Tana, arrived in the United States from Japan in 1928 at the age of 27. In March 1942, while serving at a temple in Lompoc, California, Reverend Tana was picked up by authorities who took him to the Tuna Canyon Detention Station near Los Angeles.

He was transferred from Tuna Canyon and spent the remainder of the war at U.S. Department of Justice camps in New Mexico. He diligently recorded his confinement experience, and his diary has become a valuable resource for students, historians and researchers.

Initial Procedures [3/14/1942]

The camp was completely isolated from the outside world, and the only lights that illuminated the darkness were those inside our rooms. When I look up at the clock, it was 7 a.m. Despite that hour, those around me were already chatting rather loudly about the war. Now that we are here, perhaps no one cares what we say.

We were provided with black coffee and oatmeal on a rectangular shaped dish. Not quite satisfying, we all partook of some botamochi (a Japanese sweet made with rice and red bean) that Mr. Hotta brought last night as left overs from lunch that he had had on his way to the camp. This botamochi was cut in half to feed the twelve of us.

I had heard no lunch would be served, so I forced myself to eat the oatmeal. We were told that each individual should wash and return their own dishes. Around 9 a.m., visitors were allowed to meet with the detainees in the camp and they brought us some food. I laughed at myself and would not have forced down the oatmeal had I known about this. At noon, someone brought some Hinomaru ("circle of the sun" flag of Japan) rice balls [a pickled red plum in white rice], and we gobbled those down. Regardless of whom you know, everyone here already lives like a family. At 2 p.m., family visitations were allowed.

I saw some acquaintances, including Mrs. Shimakawa, so I asked her to give a letter to [my wife] Tomoe. Paradoxically, it made me less anxious not to have any guests.

Around 3 p.m., we were placed into armed truck and driven to the CCC Camp at Tujunga on the outskirts of Los Angeles. It was raining during this transfer, and we finally arrived at the camp at 5:30 p.m.

The camp was surrounded by barbed wire fences almost 20-feet high. We went through luggage inspection, and I was assigned to Barrack F. Dinner tonight was a Japanese meal and included hot miso soup. I felt so relieved while eating it.

There was an inspection/count of the Japanese at 8:30 p.m., and lights were off at 10 p.m. I recited Buddhist texts quietly on my bed in the dark. It was too cold to fall asleep, but I slept well after wrapping my body in a blanket.

"Living in this collective and ordered environment made me think of regimented military life. We had to stay 10 feet away from the barbed wire fence. Being cut off from the outside is the most painful thing about being in camp."

From the diary of Reverend Daisho Tana
March 15, 1942

SASABUNE SASAKI

Sasabune Sasaki diary
Yokuryujo Seikatsuki (1950)
translated by Yoko Mansfield

Shuichi Sasaki was an *Issei* pioneer who arrived in America from Japan in 1905 at the age of 22. He became a respected poet, teacher, and journalist, writing under the name "Sasabune Sasaki." To support his wife, Sadie, and four children, he also worked as a life insurance salesman.

On December 7, 1941, he was arrested and went from county jail to Terminal Island, and then to Tuna Canyon Detention Station. His bilingual capabilities led to his selection as a group supervisor and translator for TCDS first officer Merrill Scott. Sasaki detailed his wartime experience in a diary that was published in 1950, and partly translated in 2015 and 2016.

"All of us had been moved around throughout the night without much sleep, so many of us just lay or sat down on the concrete floor."

Sasabune Sasaki
Diary entry, Chapter 11

Chapter 11. Then to Terminal Island

I do not know exactly when the county jail had been built, but it seemed quite new and well furnished with various facilities. The waiting room where we were herded into was very clean, sanitary, and spacious beyond compare to the police sub-station jail in which some of us had been put at first. It must have been used only for men: that there were eleven urinals, though without any partitioning screen, there was a drinking fountain, and a built-in bench. That was all the fixtures in this room.

There was another group of about 30 people brought into this room from the west area of Los Angeles, and some people from our group had been taken to some place else.

There was a steam heater, but the room was not very warm. Maybe because it was still early morning. All of us had been moved around throughout the night without much sleep, so many of us just lay or sat down on the concrete floor. I tried to lie down since I was exhausted from fatigue and sleepiness; however, as soon as I started to doze, a bodyache and a chill tormented me that I could not sleep nor rest my limbs.

Someone kept smoking cigarettes vacantly sitting on the narrow bench. Another paced back and forth inside this room. Some chatted in groups of three or five, but by this time we all had shared about our arrest or a war story of a thrilling air raid, that no loud or cheerful voice was heard. On the contrary, some were casting their eyes down in a manner of being sunk in thought. They might have been worrying about their family or supposing what would happen next to them.

Meanwhile the noise of the trains that went through the city started to be frequent and the window facing the courtyard grew lighter. The people who had been lying on the floor started to get up one by one, and the ones who had been sitting on the floor started to stand up or move to the bench. The atmosphere became a little more lively than before.

Courtesy of Mimi Sasaki

WHAT WAS IT LIKE BEING AN ENEMY ALIEN?

Shinsuke and Misao Sugimoto at Hoover Dam, 1941
Courtesy of the Sugimoto family

Postcard from Shinsuke to Misao Sugimoto from Tuna Canyon Detention Station, stamped March 2, 1942, prior to him being moved to Santa Fe Internment Camp.
Courtesy of the Sugimoto family

> "Take care everybody, avoid quarrels, live without worry, not to think so deep, live like a happy family."
>
> Shinsuke "Sam" Sugimoto

SCAN THIS QR CODE TO READ A MORE COMPLETE BIOGRAPHY OF SHINSUKE SUGIMOTO

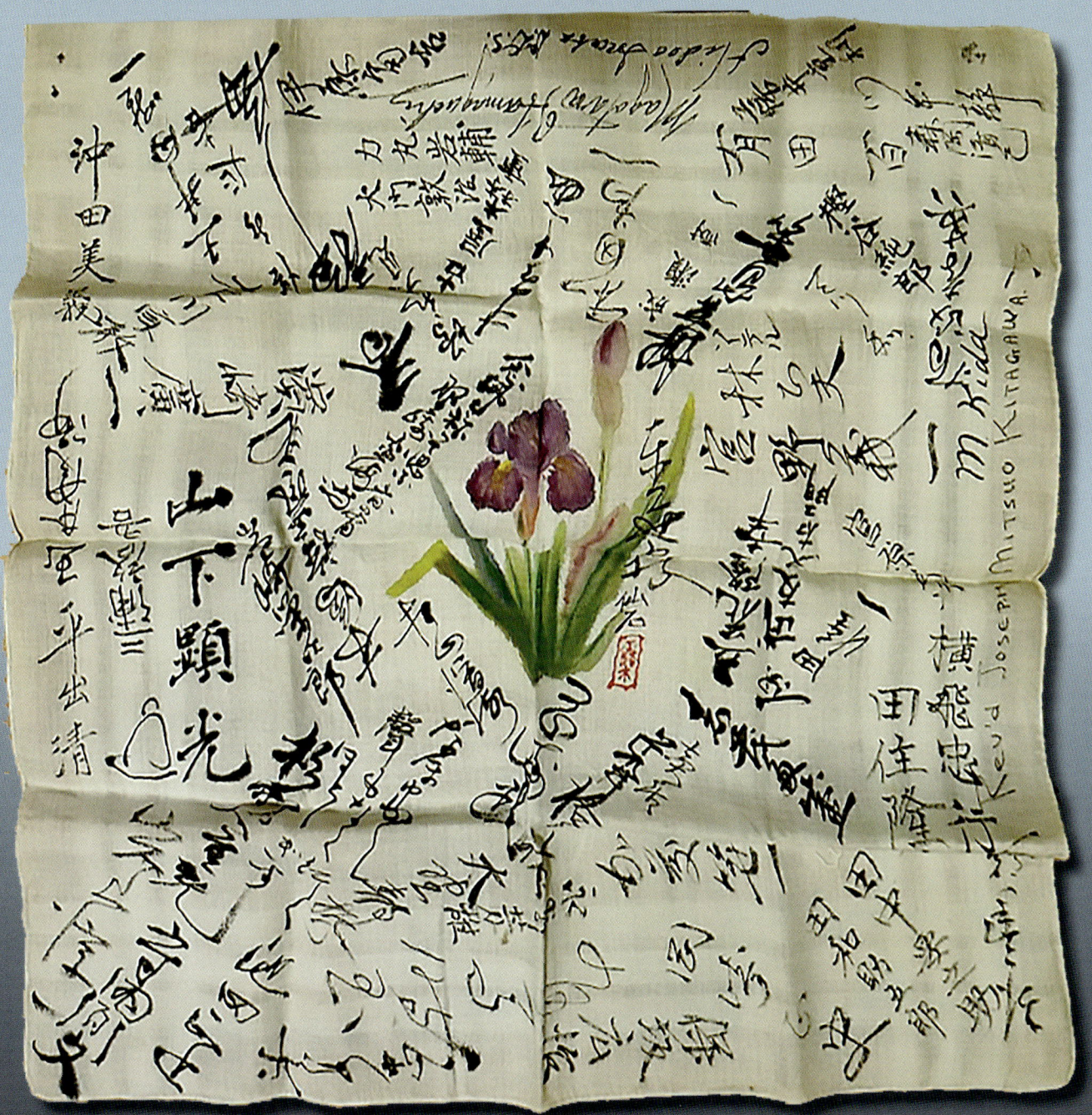

One of three handkerchiefs that Shinsuke Sugimoto had signed by internees at Santa Fe internment camp. Among the names are several who had come there from Tuna Canyon Detention Station.

Courtesy of the Sugimoto family

JAPANESE ALIENS

Japan's attack on Pearl Harbor on December 7, 1941 was an event that would forever alter the lives of Japanese in the United States.

Long-held anti-Japanese sentiment exacerbated by fear and suspicion triggered actions against persons of Japanese ancestry. During the early months of the war, many *Issei* community leaders – including priests, ministers, heads of community organizations, journalists, Japanese language teachers, businessmen, and fishermen – were picked up by FBI and other law enforcement agents, pursuant to Presidential Proclamation 2525.

Many individuals were initially held in local jails or similar facilities before being transferred to places like the Tuna Canyon Detention Station. Most would later be sent to Department of Justice (DOJ) and Army internment camps.

On February 19, 1942, President Franklin D. Roosevelt signed Executive Order 9066, allowing the military to exclude or restrict any person from designated military areas without due process for reasons of "military necessity." In the ensuing months, 120,000 persons of Japanese ancestry, two-thirds of them American-born U.S. citizens, were herded into detention centers and later incarcerated in ten War Relocation Authority (WRA) concentration camps. Most lost their homes, treasured personal belongings, pets, jobs, and livelihoods.

Many *Issei* imprisoned in DOJ or Army camps were later allowed to rejoin their families held in WRA camps. Families were also transferred from WRA camps to the DOJ camp at Crystal City, TX.

The first Japanese internees at Fort Lincoln were aliens mainly from the Terminal Island area in Los Angeles. Arrested on December 7 and 8, 1941, they were sent across country in prison trains, and unloaded under armed guard on December 18, 1941.
Courtesy John Christgau

Over 1,500 *Issei* and their *Nisei* children were used in the two hostage exchanges for U.S. citizens held by Japan during the war.

After years of hard-fought litigation, legislative efforts, and public education and mobilization, the Japanese American community and its supporters secured the passage of the Civil Liberties Act of 1988. The U.S. government issued a public acknowledgment, individual apology letters, monetary compensation, and established a public education fund as redress for the civil liberties violations resulting from the government's wartime policies. This redress was restricted to former prisoners who were U.S. citizens and legal permanent residents of Japanese ancestry and alive on the date when the legislation was passed.

Telegram announcing transfers of *Issei* from the Los Angeles County Jail to Tuna Canyon Detention Station, March 1942.
National Archives, Washington, D.C.

"We've been wanting to remind people of what happened to us and make sure the same hysteria does not overtake the leadership and the communities."

Dr. Satsuki Ina
Los Angeles Times, April 11, 2016

WHAT WAS IT LIKE BEING AN ENEMY ALIEN?

GERMAN ALIENS

Events unfolded quickly for Germans living in the United States following Japan's attack on Pearl Harbor. Within hours of the bombing on December 7, 1941, the FBI and other law enforcement authorities arrested hundreds of German immigrants.

On December 8, President Franklin Delano Roosevelt signed Presidential Proclamation 2526. Over 300,000 German immigrants were labeled "enemy aliens." Three days later, on December 11, the U.S. declared war against Germany. Thousands of German immigrants were arrested in subsequent months.

About 140 Germans from Southern California, were among those imprisoned at Tuna Canyon Detention Station. By the end of the war, at least 11,000 German immigrants and their families, including U.S.-born children, were interned in Department of Justice and U.S. Army camps in Texas (Crystal City, Kenedy, and Seagoville), Florida (Camp Blanding), Oklahoma (Stringtown), Florida (Camp Blanding), North Dakota (Fort Lincoln), Tennessee (Camp Forrest).

Some children were left to fend for themselves or placed in orphanages when their parents were arrested and interned.

Executive Order 9066, issued on February 19, 1942, authorized the Secretary of War to establish military areas which led to the mass expulsion of all German, Italian, and Japanese enemy aliens from designated prohibited zones, eighty-eight of which were in California. This caused traumatic family separation and economic hardship. The Western Defense Command's proposal to remove millions of German and

Fort Lincoln Internment Camp, located south of Bismarck, North Dakota
Courtesy United Tribes Technical College

Italian enemy aliens from all military areas, including those on the East Coast, was thwarted by the U.S. President due to the possible negative impact on the war effort. In response, the U.S. Army began an individual exclusion program and issued several hundred orders to expel selected naturalized citizens of German and Italian descent from military areas.

During the war, there were at least 15 exchanges of over 2,650 German enemy aliens and their U.S.-born family members for U.S. citizens held in Germany. Exchanged families faced hunger, forced labor, Nazi persecution, and Allied bombing as they struggled to survive.

Former internees of German ancestry in the U.S. and from Latin America, their families, and supporters continue to educate the public about U.S. wartime policies that led to internment, repatriation, and exchange of civilians of German ethnicity so as to better protect the civil liberties of future vulnerable ethnic groups. To date, the U.S. government has not redressed the civil rights violations endured by the German American and Latin American communities during World War II.

A document in the possession of Dr. Eugen Banzhaf's family shows that U.S. officials often referred to interned people as "prisoners of war." Legally and technically they were "internees."

Courtesy of Dr. Sigrid Toye

WHAT WAS IT LIKE BEING AN ENEMY ALIEN? 57

ITALIAN ALIENS

Japan's attack on Pearl Harbor on December 7, 1941 immediately affected the Italian American community as the FBI and other law enforcement officials descended on homes and businesses to arrest hundreds of Italian community leaders without charges, trials, or explanations to family members.

On December 8, Presidential Proclamation 2527 was signed, turning all Italian immigrants – more than 600,000 – into "enemy aliens." On December 11, the U.S. declared war on Italy, and arrests of Italian continued. Specifically targeted were journalists, leaders of community organizations, language school teachers, and World War I veterans.

After arrest, the enemy aliens were soon detained in facilities operated by the Immigration and Naturalization Service. During its existence, Tuna Canyon Detention Station held over 100 Italian aliens, most from Southern California.

All arrested enemy aliens eventually had hearings before civilian boards. During the hearings, aliens were not allowed to have attorneys, question witnesses, examine any evidence, or have the right to appeal. Recommendations were delivered to the U.S. Attorney General for final decisions, either unconditional release, parole, or internment. Many Italians were issued orders for internment in camps located in the South, tearing apart families.

Italians endured special registration and restrictions that were imposed on all enemy aliens. These included being required to carry enemy alien identification certificates; handing over personal property deemed contraband; staying within a five mile radius of home; obeying a curfew from 8pm to 6am daily (applied only on the West Coast); and surviving with frozen bank accounts. Italian as well as Japanese fishermen had their fishing boats

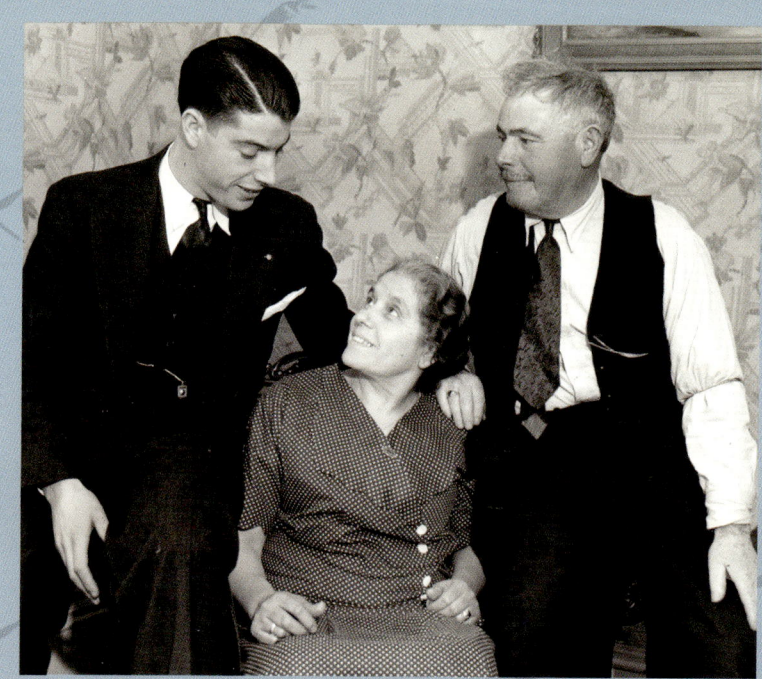

Joe DiMaggio with his parents. DiMaggio's father was a fisherman who lost his boat and his livelihood because of conditions imposed on enemy aliens.

Courtesy San Francisco History Center, San Francisco Public Library

seized by the government, which devastated livelihoods.

As authorized under Executive Order 9066, the mass exclusion of enemy aliens from prohibited zones included 10,000 Italians living in California, many of whom were elderly women. These individuals were forcibly separated from their families, homes, and businesses with less than one month's notice.

In October 1942, restrictions were lifted on Italian aliens. Factors in this decision may have included concern for the Italian American vote in upcoming Congressional elections, their support for the war effort as the U.S. prepared to invade Italy, and complaints from Italian American troops about the treatment of their parents. Policies for Italian excludees and internees remained in place until the armistice with Italy in September 1943. By that time, over 1800 Italians had been interned and at least 37 were shipped to Europe in an hostage exchange.

In 2000, the U.S. Congress passed the Wartime Violation of Italian American Civil Liberties Act. As ordered by the Act, the U.S. Attorney General submitted a report, *A Review of the Restrictions on Persons of Italian Ancestry During WWII*, to Congress in November 2001. Despite this report, the U.S. government has not granted an apology or redress to former internees of Italian ancestry.

Page 1

Section 3(7) - A list of ports from which fishermen of Italian ancestry were restricted *

Naval District	Port
1st Naval District	Boston, Massachusetts
	Gloucester, Massachusetts
	Portsmouth, New Hampshire
	Newport, Rhode Island
3rd Naval District	New Haven, Connecticut
	New London, Connecticut
	New York, New York
4th Naval District	Wilmington, Delaware
	Philadelphia, Pennsylvania
5th Naval District	Washington, District Of Columbia
	Annapolis, Maryland
	Baltimore, Maryland
	Norfolk, Virginia
	Portsmouth, Virginia
6th Naval District	Savannah, Georgia
	Wilmington, North Carolina
	Charleston, South Carolina
7th Naval District	Jacksonville, Florida
	Key West, Florida
	Miami, Florida
8th Naval District	Pensacola, Florida
	New Orleans, Louisiana
	Galveston, Texas
11th Naval District	Long Beach, California
	San Diego, California
	San Pedro, California
12th Naval District	California City, California
	Eureka, California
	Monterey, California
	Richmond, California
	San Francisco, California
13th Naval District	Bremerton, Washington
	Seattle, Washington

* Only the major ports within each naval district are listed, although smaller ports may have been affected. A comprehensive list of ports associated with each naval district during World War II could not be found, even after extensive research. The naval districts listed here represent the coastal districts in the contiguous United States; other districts, such as the 9th, 10th, and 14th districts, were either non-contiguous or interior districts. A 2nd Naval District did not exist.

UNITED STATES DEPARTMENT OF JUSTICE
REPORT TO THE CONGRESS OF THE UNITED STATES
A REVIEW OF THE RESTRICTIONS ON PERSONS OF ITALIAN ANCESTRY DURING WORLD WAR II
Appendix G
November, 2001

LATIN AMERICAN ALIENS

The existence of Japanese, Germans, and Italians residing throughout Latin America posed a predicament for the United States, which was concerned about possible Nazi infiltration and the danger this might pose for western hemispheric security.

Following the Japanese attack on Pearl Harbor on December 7, 1941, the U.S. government initiated the seizure and deportation of approximately 6,600 men, women, and children (both immigrant residents and children) of Japanese, German, and Italian descent from thirteen Central and South American countries and two Caribbean nations.

Ship transport to the U.S. was arduous. Visas were not issued and identity papers and the passengers' passports were confiscated. These individuals were labeled illegal aliens and considered "potentially dangerous."

One ship, the USAT Puebla, docked at San Pedro, California on February 10, 1943 with 316 men, women, and children aboard. Some 207 of them were processed into Tuna Canyon Detention Station.

After Japan's surrender in September 1945, the U.S. government authorized the forced deportation of 1,400 enemy aliens of Japanese ancestry to Japan. More than 300 Japanese Peruvians fought deportation and were paroled out of the camps, sponsored by Japanese American relatives, churches, and/or economic guarantors (as cheap labor). About 100 Japanese Peruvians were permitted to return to Peru.

Meanwhile, about 1,000 persons of German ancestry petitioned to return to their homes in Latin America. Several years passed before the remaining internees would be released and allowed to return to their former countries of residence.

The Refugee Relief Act of 1953 was amended to allow Latin American internees remaining in the U.S. to apply to change their illegal alien status to legal permanent residents. Many later became American citizens.

As part of the settlement of the *Mochizuki vs. United States of America* court case, the U.S. publicly acknowledged that government action had wrongfully interned individuals from Latin America during World War II and granted $5,000 in reparations to each person of Japanese ancestry deemed eligible for the payment. However, the controversial redress action did not extend to German, Jewish, and Italian internees.

The U.S. government has yet to officially apologize for its wartime actions that resulted in denying rights to internees from Latin America.

Following fathers, sons, and husbands into internment these women and children asked permission to accompany their male relatives arrested as enemy aliens. Of Japanese, German and Italian nationalities, they are leaving an internment camp in the Panama Canal Zone for the United States and another internment camp there. Utmost secrecy prevailed in evacuation of the group to protect them from their own submarines.

*San Francisco History Center,
San Francisco Public Library*

Japanese Peruvians in the Panama Canal Zone en route to U.S. internment camps. April 2, 1942.

*U.S. Army Signal Corps Photo.
National Archives. Courtesy of NJAHS.*

WHAT WAS IT LIKE BEING AN ENEMY ALIEN?

COULD DETENTION/ INTERNMENT HAPPEN TODAY?

This book explores how the civil and human rights of over 2,000 people were violated at Tuna Canyon Detention Station. This is just one part of a larger picture that included tens of thousands of additional enemy aliens from the United States and Latin America and the subsequent incarceration of 120,000 Americans of Japanese descent, both aliens and citizens.

For all of the groups involved, what happened during World War II was preceded by histories of prejudice and discrimination – factors which contributed to public and political support for the government's actions.

Civil and human rights are guaranteed by the U.S. Constitution and other documents, but these rights can be empty promises. They become real only to the degree that people are willing to fight to uphold these principles.

In today's world, there are increasing threats to internal security. And unfortunately, many people are fearful of groups with which they are not very familiar. This can easily lead to misunderstandings.

The legal basis for enemy alien detention and internment during World War II still exists. More recently, the 2012 National Defense Authorization Act potentially allows the government to arrest and indefinitely detain, without due process, American citizens merely suspected of terrorist activity.

Lessons from the past, including those from Tuna Canyon Detention Station, are important to prevent abuses of power against specific groups, such as those that occurred during World War II.

We should never repeat these mistakes.

This project was funded, in part, by a grant from the U.S. Department of the Interior, National Park Service, Japanese American Confinement Sites Grant Program. Any opinions, findings, and conclusions or recommendations expressed in this material are those of the author(s) and do not necessarily reflect the views of the U.S. Department of the Interior.

This material received Federal financial assistance for the preservation and interpretation of U.S. confinement sites where Japanese Americans were detained during World War II. Under Title VI of the Civil Rights Act of 1964, Section 504 of the Rehabilitation Act of 1973, and the Age Discrimination Act of 1975, as amended, the U.S. Department of Interior prohibits discrimination on the basis of race, color, national origin, disability or age in its federally funded assisted projects. If you believe you have been discriminated against in any program, activity, or facility as described above, or if you desire further information, please write to:

Office of Equal Opportunity

National Park Service

1849 C Street, NW

Washington, DC 20240.